Meet the DENVER BRONCOS

BY
ZACK BURGESS

NORWOODHOUSE PRESS

CHICAGO, ILLINOIS

NORWOOD HOUSE 🏠 PRESS

P.O. Box 316598 • Chicago, Illinois 60631
For more information about Norwood House Press please visit our website at
www.norwoodhousepress.com or call 866-565-2900.

Photo Credits:
  All photos courtesy of Associated Press, except for the following: Topps, Inc. (6, 10 both, 11 all, 18),
  Black Book Archives (7, 22), Fleer Corp. (23).

  Cover Photo: Kevin Terrell/Associated Press

  The football memorabilia photographed for this book is part of the authors' collection. The collectibles used
  for artistic background purposes in this series were manufactured by many different card companies—
  including Bowman, Donruss, Fleer, Leaf, O-Pee-Chee, Pacific, Panini America, Philadelphia Chewing Gum,
  Pinnacle, Pro Line, Pro Set, Score, Topps, and Upper Deck—as well as several food brands, including
  Crane's, Hostess, Kellogg's, McDonald's and Post.

Designer: Ron Jaffe
Series Editors: Mike Kennedy and Mark Stewart
Project Management: Black Book Partners, LLC.
Editorial Production: Lisa Walsh

LIBRARY OF CONGRESS CATALOGING-IN-PUBLICATION DATA
    Names: Burgess, Zack.
    Title: Meet the Denver Broncos / by Zack Burgess.
    Description: Chicago, Illinois : Norwood House Press, [2016] | Series: Big
       picture sports | Includes bibliographical references and index. |
       Audience: Grade: K to Grade 3.
    Identifiers: LCCN 2015023113| ISBN 9781599537535 (Library Edition : alk.
       paper) | ISBN 9781603578561 (eBook)
    Subjects: LCSH: Denver Broncos (Football team)--Miscellanea--Juvenile
       literature.
    Classification: LCC GV956.D37 B87 2016 | DDC 796.332/640978883--dc23
    LC record available at http://lccn.loc.gov/2015023113

288N—072016
Manufactured in the United States of America in North Mankato, Minnesota

CONTENTS

Words in **bold type** are defined on page 24.

The Broncos play with amazing energy.

Call Me a Bronco

In the Old West, the strongest cowboys were the ones who could tame wild horses. Trying to control the Denver Broncos is a much harder job. No team plays with more power and energy. The Broncos don't stop kicking until the final whistle blows.

TIME MACHINE

The Broncos helped start the **American Football League** in 1960. They joined the National Football League (NFL) 10 years later. The Broncos have always relied on great passers. **Craig Morton**, John Elway, and Peyton Manning were three of the best.

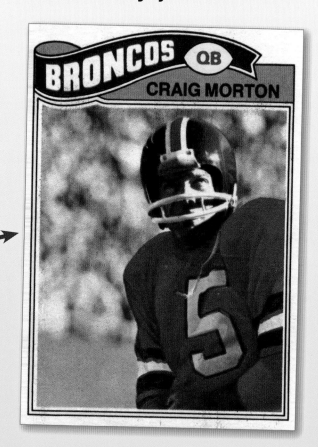

BRONCOS QB
CRAIG MORTON

John Elway drops back to pass.

7

Mile High Stadium is always packed on game day.

Best Seat in the House

The Broncos play in Mile High Stadium. It replaced an old stadium with the same name. Denver has thin air. This gives the Broncos a big advantage. Late in games, opposing teams are often tired out. But the Broncos are still full of energy.

SHOE BOX

The trading cards on these pages show some of the best Broncos ever.

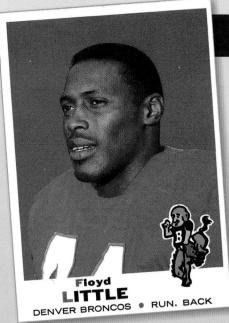

FLOYD LITTLE

RUNNING BACK · 1967-1975

Floyd was voted team captain of the Broncos in his first year. He was an **All-Pro** in 1969.

TOM JACKSON

LINEBACKER · 1973-1986

Tom always got the best out of his teammates. He led Denver's "Orange Crush" defense in the 1970s.

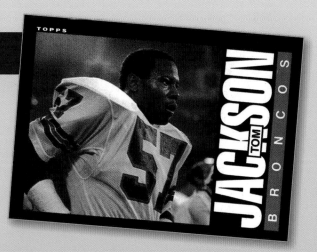

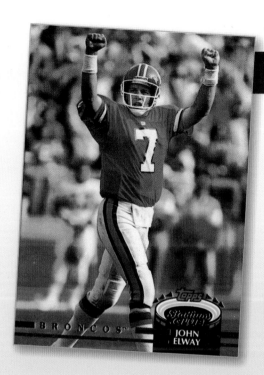

JOHN ELWAY

QUARTERBACK · 1983-1998

John could throw a touchdown pass from anywhere on the field. He led the Broncos to two Super Bowl wins.

STEVE ATWATER

SAFETY · 1989-1998

Steve may have been the hardest-hitting safety in NFL history. He was an All-Pro in 1991 and 1992.

PEYTON MANNING

QUARTERBACK · 2012 TO 2015

Peyton was the NFL's Most Valuable Player in 2013. Two seasons later, he led the Broncos to their third Super Bowl victory.

THE BIG PICTURE

Look at the two photos on page 13. Both appear to be the same. But they are not. There are three differences. Can you spot them?

Answers on page 23.

12

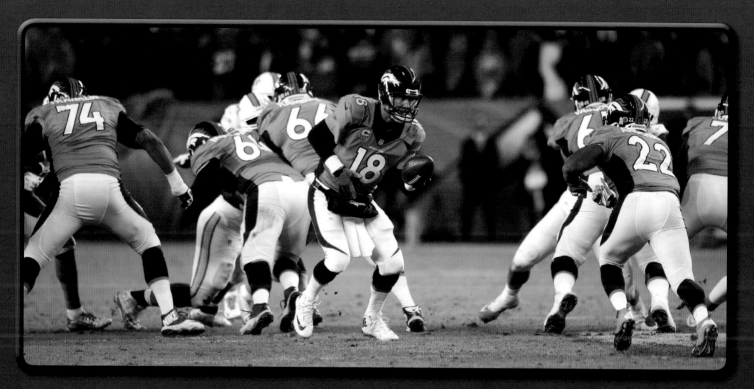

TRUE OR FALSE?

Shannon Sharpe was a star tight end. Two of these facts about him are **TRUE**. One is **FALSE**. Do you know which is which?

1. Shannon's older brother, Sterling, was a star receiver for the Green Bay Packers.

2. Shannon owns a company called the Sharpe Image.

3. Shannon caught 55 touchdown passes for the Broncos.

Answer on page 23.

Shannon Sharpe celebrates a touchdown.

Denver fans love their Broncos.

Go Broncos, Go!

Broncos fans are loud and proud. The stadium is a sea of orange on game days. When the visiting team misses a pass, the fans yell "in-com-PLETE." Then the *wuh-wuh* sound of a "sad" trombone plays over the stadium speakers.

ON THE MAP

Here is a look at where five Broncos were born, along with a fun fact about each.

1 DENNIS SMITH · SANTA MONICA, CALIFORNIA
Dennis had 30 **interceptions** with the Broncos.

2 RICH JACKSON · NEW ORLEANS, LOUISIANA
Rich was nicknamed "Tombstone" for the way he buried opponents.

3 RANDY GRADISHAR · WARREN, OHIO ●────────────────▶

Randy was an All-Pro in 1977 and 1978.

4 FRANK TRIPUCKA · BLOOMFIELD, NEW JERSEY
Frank joined the Broncos as a coach in 1960 … and then became their quarterback!

5 TIM TEBOW · MAKATI, PHILIPPINES
In 2011, Tim led Denver to the **playoffs** for the first time in six seasons.

BRONCOS

AFC PRO BOWL
RANDY
GRADISHAR   ILB

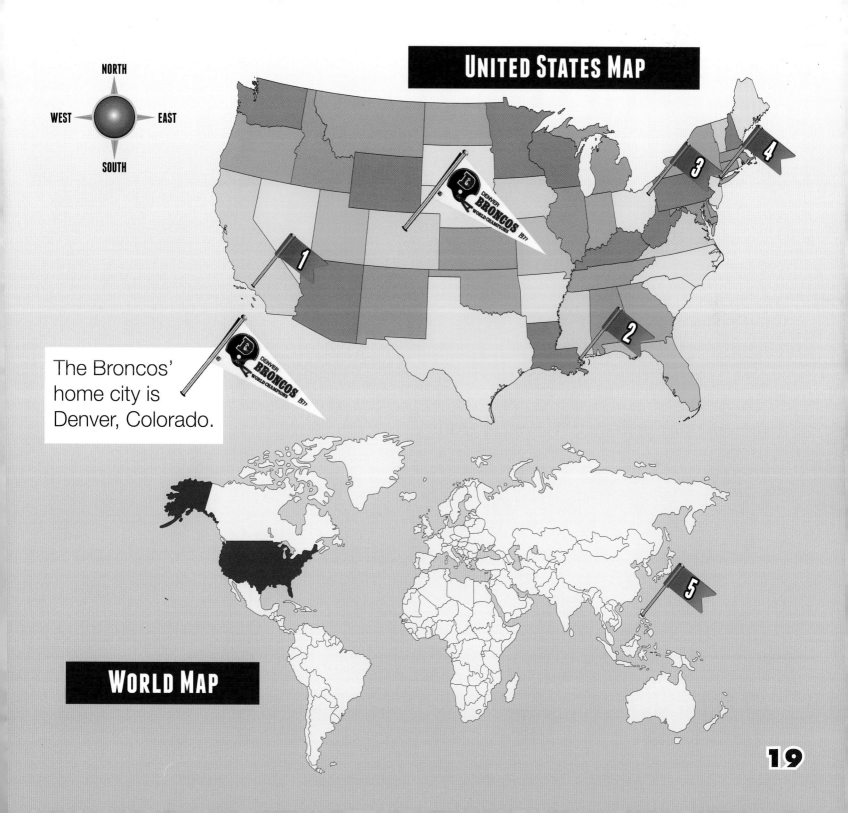

UNITED STATES MAP

NORTH

WEST — EAST

SOUTH

The Broncos' home city is Denver, Colorado.

WORLD MAP

Von Miller wears the Broncos' home uniform.

Football teams wear different uniforms for home and away games. The main colors of the Broncos are orange and blue. The team also has special all-blue uniforms.

DeMarcus Ware wears the Broncos' away uniform.

The Broncos' helmet is blue. It has a cartoon bronco on each side. The team's main color in the early 1960s was brown. The Broncos changed after the players complained it was bad luck.

We Won!

The Broncos are one of a few teams to win the Super Bowl two years in a row. They were NFL champs in 1997 and 1998. Terrell Davis and **John Elway** were the stars of those teams. Von Miller led the Broncos to their third Super Bowl win in 2016.

RECORD BOOK

These Broncos set team records.

TOUCHDOWN PASSES	RECORD
Season: Peyton Manning (2013)	55
Career: John Elway	300

RUSHING YARDS	RECORD
Season: **Terrell Davis** (1998)	2,008
Career: Terrell Davis	7,607

INTERCEPTIONS	RECORD
Season: Goose Gonsulin (1960)	11
Career: Steve Foley	44

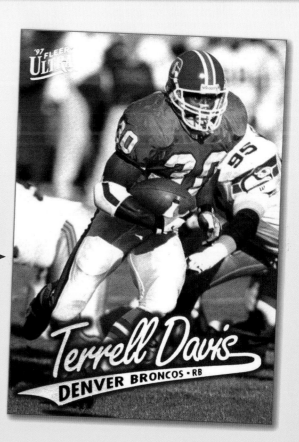

Football Words

All-Pro
An honor given to the best NFL player at each position.

American Football League
A rival league of the NFL that played from 1960 to 1969.

Interceptions
Passes caught by a defensive player.

Playoffs
The games played after the regular season that decide which teams will play in the Super Bowl.

Index

Photos are on **BOLD** numbered pages.

About the Author

Zack Burgess has been writing about sports for more than 20 years. He has lived all over the country and interviewed lots of All-Pro football players, including Brett Favre, Eddie George, Jerome Bettis, Shannon Sharpe, and Rich Gannon. Zack was the first African American beat writer to cover Major League Baseball when he worked for the *Kansas City Star*.

About the Broncos

Learn more at these websites:

www.denverbroncos.com • www.profootballhof.com
www.teamspiritextras.com/Overtime/html/broncos.html